How Love Got Started

Love Is What It Does

Gwendolyn B. Frazier Elmore

Verses marked KJV are taken from The Holy Bible, King James Version. Copyright © 2009 by Zondervan All rights reserved.

Verses marked NKJV are taken from the New King James Version. Copyright © 1979, 1980, 1982 by Thomas Nelson, Inc. All rights reserved.

All the stories in this book are real life accounts and all the names used are real people.

All rights reserved. No part of this book may be reproduced or transmitted in any form or by any means without written permission from author.

ISBN 978-0-615-83348-4
Published by Truly In His Hands

NEW RELEASES

Forgive – It's The Gift That Keeps You Living

-"Forgive It's The Gift That Keeps You Living" explains why God requires us to forgive others in order to receive any of God's promises. Our forgiving is a gift we give to ourselves.

Hugs - Bring Healing

"Hugs – Bring Healing" explains the health benefits of a hug and how its positive effects still baffle the science community.

These books when read together, help explain how the relationships we have with others impact how we receive from God.

http://trulyinhishands.wix.com/themarriagecoach

To order visit www.amazon.com

About the front cover:

Picture of our father Dr. Elder Patrick Frazier, Sr. at age 82.

Hands forming a heart are the hands of my husband, Eugene with our granddaughter Michelle Renae's feet, signifying the legacy of love and protection of family continues through generations.

Dr. Elder Patrick, Sr. and Minister Cora Lee "MaDear" Cohen Frazier

DEDICATION

This book is dedicated to my parents, the late Dr. Patrick Frazier and the late Mrs. Cora L. Cohen Frazier. They taught me and my siblings by example how to love and forgive. I thank them for showing us that we can experience marriage and family the way God intended. Our parents celebrated 58 years of marriage before Daddy passed away on August 1, 2004.

This book's contents are written in honor of their memory and with the hope of continuing their legacy with the five words that were one of my father's favorite sayings, "Love is What It Does."

A Letter to my Heavenly Father

Dear Father,

Thank you Father for placing the desire to write this book for others to know the life lessons that have been learned to help us strive for a Godly marriage that leaves a legacy for our children. Lessons on loving and forgiving have afforded us a head start on problems in our relationships as they occurred. We learned that, no matter what, we have the choice to keep loving and keep forgiving.

Thank you for allowing us to be born into this family, Dr. Patrick and Minister Cora Lee (Cohen) Frazier. You knew the plans that you had for our lives even before we were even formed in our mother's womb. We would not be who we are today if we had not received the strong foundation that was laid for us. Father, thank you for giving us an earthly father who showed his children the love of a father. Thank you for a father who displayed your love and loved unconditionally in spite of what others may have thought. It is that love that has enabled us to trust you as Father.

Thank you for placing the desire to write this book and share with others the upbringing that has kept us sane during times of trouble and when we needed to just walk out your Word.

TABLE OF CONTENTS

FOREWORD	8
INTRODUCTION	9
What is Love?	13
Opposites Do Attract	21
Love Is What It Does	35
Their Quiver Is Full of Them	39
Called to Serve	54
Miracles Do Happen	59
And God Blessed Them	76
How to Get From Where You Are	80
Prayers	83
Special Thanks to Some Very Special People	95

FOREWORD

How Love Got Started challenges the traditional concept of love in the family as a passive presence and shows how love is an active force that drives the family. For the Frazier family, love does not merely endure the hardships of life, instead love is harnessed as an active driving force that directs everything from the dynamics of family relationships, the structure of the household, the policies of the household, and even how a family views the world beyond the household.

1 Corinthians 13:4-8 is a popular Scripture about love being patient and kind, but few understand how to activate the power of its words in their lives. *How Love Got Started* illustrates the power of these verses when it serves as the pulse of a family. The Frazier family's story is a practical illustration of love not only as a mindset but also as an action.

This book should not be taken for granted because its pages are filled with solid principles that can help transform your household from a place where love is not to where love can be with the expression that *How Love Got Started*.

Dr. Johnathan Briggs, Senior Pastor
Truth and Fellowship Global Outreach Ministry

INTRODUCTION

I have been inspired to write this book to help the Body of Christ strengthen marriages and family relationships. I believe that before the family can be whole, there are some prerequisites to getting the husband/father and the wife/ mother roles in proper order. Women have taken on the role of leading the family spiritually but it is not their total responsibility. The husband is the head of the family and the wife is the help meet. It takes both fulfilling their roles for success.

We have all been given many definitions of love, but what is it really? How many of us have been caught up into thinking that a person loves us when they do everything we want them to? God never intended for us to get caught up into anyone else's perception of love but His. Too often we do this without examining the Word of God to see what He is really saying.

Husbands, love your wives, even as Christ also loved the church, and gave himself for it.
Ephesians 5:25KJV

For God so love the world that He gave his only begotten Son;
John 3:16a KJV

What an unselfish act of love - a love that keeps loving. It is my sincere prayer that, upon completing this book with your spouse, you will understand the importance of living God's way and use this book to maintain your marriage and family relationships. To help you apply these principles to your relationships, each chapter concludes with questions and a 30 day challenge. You shouldn't feel obligated to complete the activities, but they are designed to help you apply the concepts you read to your present family circumstances.

Even though every marriage is not the same, the principles for marriage, according to the Word of God, are the same. This is a universal scripture.

This book of the law shall not depart out of your mouth; but thou shalt meditate therein day and night, that thou mayest observe to do according to all that is written therein: for then thou shalt make thy way prosperous, and then thou shalt have good success.
Joshua 1:8 KJV

It is a matter of choice to begin to use God's Word as a guide and to seek out others that are successful in doing so.

In the beginning God created man and woman to live together with one another as husband and wife and, through marriage, to bring children into this world.

God gave Adam a wife because she provided what He could not, companionship. God's plan is for the man to be the head and for the woman to be his "help meet" to fulfill their assignment on earth. In the book of Genesis, we were instructed to be fruitful (increase) multiply (make more, be in authority or excel).

It is important that husbands and wives get marriage right for generations to come so that God's plan becomes the plan for the family.

Likewise, ye husbands, dwell with them according to knowledge, giving honour unto the wife, as unto the weaker vessel, and as being heirs together of the grace of life; that your prayers be not hindered.
1 Peter 3:7 KJV

The husband and wife are heirs together of the grace of life and should exemplify equality and a partnership. It takes a male and a female, that is a man born male and a woman born female to fulfill God's original plan for marriage. You both are in this together, and it can't be done successfully without a committed effort from both parties. Belief in the saying, "Marriage is 50/50" is why so many marriages fail. Spouses have to agree to put 100 percent in to reap the benefits that God says we are to enjoy.

And the Lord God said, It is not good that the man should be alone; I will make him a help meet for him.

Genesis 2:18 KJV

Marriage has been designed to meet our basic human need for companionship is one of the benefits.

Marriage is honorable in all, and the bed is undefiled.

Hebrews 13:4 KJV

Another benefit is that it has been designed for pure and undefiled sexual fulfillment.

Knowing how important marriage is to God will help your partner and you understand that it was created by God for His purpose.

What is Love?

[Love] suffereth long, and is kind; [love] envieth not; [love] vaunteth not itself, is not puffed up, Doth not behave itself unseemingly, seeketh not her own, is not easily provoked, thinketh no evil; Rejoiceth not in iniquity, but rejoiceth in the truth; Beareth all things, believeth all things, hopeth all things, endureth all things. [Love] never faileth: but whether there be prophecies, they shall fail; whether there be tongues, they shall cease; whether there be knowledge, it shall vanish away.
1 Corinthians 13:4-8 KJV

Love is so important to God that it is mentioned over 60,000 times in the Bible. This suggests that we need to find out more about this love thing to really begin to operate in it as God instructs us!

Be ye therefore followers of God, as dear children; And walk in love, as Christ also hath loved us, and hath given himself for us an offering and sacrifice to God for a sweet-smelling savor.
Ephesians 5:1-2 KJV

1 Corinthians 13:4-8 breaks down love into seven traits that love is and seven traits that love is not. The goal is to teach the Body of Christ **how** to love.
This next Scripture focuses on how the Body of Christ is called to love.

But ye shall receive power, after that the Holy Ghost is come upon you: and ye shall be witnesses unto me both in Jerusalem, and in all Judea, and in Samaria, and unto the uttermost part of the earth.
Acts 1:8 KJV

We have been instructed to be witnesses of God's power and love in Jerusalem (home), Judea (community & church), Samaria (our state) and unto the uttermost part of the earth (all the world).

How are we to effectively love others when we can't walk in love toward the people with whom we live daily? When we can walk in love toward the people we live with, then we can do it outside our homes. Love is not always automatic, it is a choice. We can make a decision to walk in love. You may wonder, "How can I walk in love when I haven't seen it displayed?"

This book of the law shall not depart out of thy mouth; but thou shalt meditate therein day and night, that thou mayest observe to do according to all that is written therein: for then shalt make thy way prosperous, and then thou shalt have good success.

Joshua 1:8 KJV

It all starts with hearing the Word on love and then meditating (mutter, repeat over and over, keep our mind on) on the Scriptures about love. We are creatures of habit, so many times we conform to what we saw in our families and some of it was totally against the Word of God. We must transform our minds from what we saw and heard that does not line up with the Word of God. Walking in love has to begin with spending time with God in His presence and practicing what the Word says concerning love in our homes so that we will be ready to be witnesses in our community, church, state, and the world.

A new commandment I give unto you, That ye love one another; as I have loved you, that ye also love one another.

John 13:34 KJV

The Hebrew word for love is "Ahav," which means to be fond of, to delight in, to desire, to like, and to desire to be in the presence of. It implies an ardent and vehement inclination of the mind and a tenderness of affection at the same time. Love is so important that our faith does not work without it. We want to use faith (the Word) for material things, but do we understand how faith really works?

But faith which worketh by love.

Galatians 5:6b KJV

Without love, the Word won't work. Faith will not work if love is not present. Love must be practiced daily. It must become our reason for living. We have to purposely be kind and loving toward one another, especially at home. One major problem that we have with loving others is faulted by the way we think about them (mind) causes us to feel a certain way (emotions) and then we choose the way we act toward them (will). Our mind is our thinker, our emotions are our feeler and our will is our chooser. Whenever we think, we begin to feel a certain way and then we choose to respond, or not respond, a certain way. This is why the Bible instructs us to focus our minds on lovely thoughts.

We will continue to choose to live a life of love, and our faith in the Word will continue to produce in our lives. This is why Philippians 4:8 should be incorporated as our daily confession.

Finally, brethren, whatsoever things are true, whatsoever things are honest, whatsoever things are just, whatsoever things are pure, whatsoever things are lovely, whatsoever things are of good report; if there be any virtue, and if there be any praise, think on these things. Philippians 4:8 KJV

For all have sinned, and come short of the glory of God;
Romans 3:23 KJV

Love covers a multitude of sins.
I Peter 4:8b KJV

Not only does love cause the Word to have power in our lives, but it also liberates us from the limitations that sin and shortcomings place on our lives. The Word of God lets us know that love covers a multitude of sins. That doesn't mean we cover up the sins of others, but it does mean we protect them, not expose them. When we recognize things in our spouses that need to be addressed, it needs to be done in private and with prayer. We all have character flaws that we need to work on, but don't spend so much time on finding all the flaws in your spouse that you never see those in yourself. Through prayer, change will take place. But let me warn you —**YOU WILL CHANGE FIRST**.

You could have been praying about something that your spouse may or may not be doing then one day realize you are not as bothered about that thing as you once were. My husband grew up with a single mother and I grew up in a two-parent household, so sometimes our approach toward disciplining our own children were different. His approach wasn't bad, just different from how I was trained. I had two loving parents and some things I never had to worry about because I knew the love of a father who was also a loving husband and an outstanding provider.

For example, his quick fix was teaching the children to always fight back, my approach was to talk it out. If they had someone teasing them at school his approach was to punch them out. My approach was to report it to the teacher first and let her handle it. If he/she doesn't get it resolved then report to the principal. If that doesn't work then maybe a good punch might be necessary at that point. I just stopped talking about it and one day I was at peace with it. It wasn't long before he came to me and told me that he agreed with how I said those situations should be handled.

Remember, when a married couple goes before God, He sees them as one.

> ...*they shall be one flesh*
> Genesis 2:24 KJV

Separate but as one in spirit and mind. How can we go before God and talk bad about our spouse when He sees us as one? God already knows about all of our spouse's issues. He also knows about all of the issues we have too! God puts up with things from us until we get it right, so we should be willing to do that for our spouses.

I have pleasant memories of my father honoring and respecting my mother to the point that everyone knew that when you dealt with her, you needed to be very careful not to mistreat her in any way or you would have to deal with him. Once, a man walked into a place and began using profanity and Daddy quickly responded because MaDear was present, and he didn't want that language spoken in front of her. There were also times when he sent her to complete some business transactions, and the folks knew they had better handle her correct or else Daddy would deal with them. He taught my brothers by example that wives are to be honored as the weaker, not lesser, vessel.

It was very clear that we saw I Corinthians 13 displayed in our home. Love was not selfish or selfcentered, it always took into account the family as a whole. Decisions that were made were for everyone's benefit not just my father. Daddy moved his business next door when MaDear started working so he would be home when we got home from school. Love was not puffed up or didn't behave itself unseemingly. Arguments were not something we witnessed with our parents, we never experienced them behaving out of character with each other. Our parents gave of themselves unselfishly to us and to the work of the kingdom. After a hard day's work, MaDear drove us 32 miles away to have piano lessons. Sometimes she would do it twice a week. In our family, love was a choice that was shown through action.

Writing Challenge

What did love look like in your family growing up? How was it different from the way love is described in this chapter?

What does love look like in your family now? How is it different from the way love is described in this chapter?

~~~~~~~~30 Day Challenge~~~~~~~~

1. Commit to meditating on the Scripture in this chapter daily.
2. Underline or highlight the strategies in this chapter that you are not already using and commit to using it for 30 days.

Opposites Do Attract

Daddy and MaDear were quite the odd couple. In no way, form or fashion would anyone ever think that the two of them were a perfect match. Daddy was from the streets and MaDear wasn't allowed in the streets. The lion and the lamb in spirit, they were very different but very attracted to each other.

My father, Patrick Frazier, was born December 12, 1921 to Willie and Maggie (Singletary) Frazier. Granddaddy often had him come in to the house from playing outside to read the Bible. Daddy thought his father didn't like him because he was the only child that was required to do this. This went on for many years. My grandfather didn't even profess to be "Born Again," yet God used him to train Daddy. This was the beginning of God's plan for Daddy being revealed. Daddy had no understanding at the time of why this was done, but today all my siblings and I do. Daddy was quite the Bible scholar and great teacher of God's Word because of it!

When Daddy was in the 8th grade he had to drop out of school to help his family. He enlisted in the Army/Air Force and served in WWII. Daddy was tested and had the highest I.Q. out of 300 soldiers in his unit. What an accomplishment!
He often shared stories about his tour in England with us. After serving four years, he returned home and

the beauty of Cora Lee Cohen got his attention. He was a good man, but he smoked, drank and loved dancing at the club. That was not going to work for Jim and Charlotte Cohen's baby girl. They were very protective of her, and they weren't sure if he would be the husband they wanted for her, He was never disrespectful to her or them, but he was a thug. Daddy wasn't a professed Christian but quite the opposite.

He had good work values and ethics, but he just didn't tolerate a lot of foolishness. Jim and Charlotte Cohen shared the Biblical understanding of what it takes to be a good husband.

> *Husbands, love your wives, even as Christ also loved the church, and gave himself for it; That he might sanctify and cleanse it with the washing of water by the word, That he might present it to himself a glorious church, not having spot, or wrinkle, or any such thing; but that it should be holy and without blemish. So ought men to love their wives as their own bodies. He that loveth his wife loveth himself.* Ephesians 5:25-28 KJV

Husbands have been instructed to love their wives as Christ loved the church and gave himself for it. What does that mean? Do husbands really know? Christ loved us so much that regardless of our shortcomings, He still died for us. This means that husbands should love their wives regardless of their wives' shortcomings, and this love should extend to the point of being willing to let their flesh die. We often want to choose how we love. Usually, it is the "if" syndrome. If you do this for me, then I'll do that for you. Jesus gave of himself although He was fully aware of all our faults. God's sacrifice of giving His Son for us is the best expression of love that we will ever experience. God is love, and we cannot allow ourselves to think that we don't have to love the way God does.

> *So ought men to love their wives as their own bodies. He that loveth his wife loveth himself.*
> Ephesians 5:28 KJV

Do men know what that really means? The way to tell if a husband really loves himself is by the way he treats his wife; men ought to love their wives as they love themselves. The problem with most of us is that we have not learned to truly love ourselves, that's why we can't love others how we should. We are products of what we saw love to be. Some of us received gifts to make up for the love that parents weren't able to give because they didn't know how. Many of us were introduced to the "if" syndrome as if it were love when we were told that "if you really loved me, you would do what I say," but that wasn't right. As a result, many grew up with a warped view of what love is. The Word of God says love is not selfish. When one is selfish, they are only concerned about themselves: "what I want" and, "it's all about me."

How can we get away from the wrong thinking about how to love? The first thing we need to do is to change our way of thinking, renew our minds.

And be not conformed to this world; but be ye transformed by the renewing of your mind, that ye may prove what is the good and acceptable, and perfect, will of God. Romans 12:2 KJV

Renewing of your mind to what the Word of God says concerning every area of our love for one another.

Husbands have a greater responsibility on them; they must love their wives as Christ loved the church and died for it. Men are expected to die to the flesh and live through the spirit. This love is to be continuous, not once and in a while but consistent. The opening phrase, "Husbands, love your wives," is mentioned not only in Ephesians, but again in a different Scripture. This tells us that it is of great importance.

Husbands love your wives, and be not bitter against them.
Colossians 3:19 KJV

An all knowing God knew that opportunity would present itself for that to happen, so He has instructed husbands not to be bitter towards their wives or make them (their wives) bitter. I believe that God knew there would be times when a husband may not be pleased with his wife's actions, so He gave men a command not to be bitter. There are situations in a marriage that can and will happen that could cause a bitter reaction or response but it doesn't have to. The wife could over go over the budget and it doesn't have to end in bitterness towards her. She may forget to pick up the dry cleaning. She maybe 15 minutes late picking hubby up from work. Even if she burns dinner or not prepare what you think she should have or if she bleaches your favorite jeans. Times will arise when a husband could become bitter but he can choose not to.

Husbands shouldn't hold grudges for their wives past mistakes. A quick note here; vice versa, wives should not hold grudges for their husbands past mistakes.

Daddy understood the Biblical definition of a husband because he had read and the Bible in its entirety so many times that the Word was embedded in his spirit and revelation on it. We never heard Daddy speak a harshly toward MaDear. He was always loving and kind to her. Susan says she had always admired the way Daddy treated MaDear. He never called her by her name; it was always "honey," "darling," "sugar," etc. Daddy never left home without kissing MaDear, and he always planted a kiss when he returned. As noted in Song of Solomon 1:2,

"Kiss me again and again, your love is sweeter than wine."

When a man finds a wife, he finds a good thing and obtaineth favor of the Lord.
Proverbs 18:22 KJV

MaDear, born as Cora Lee Cohen, was born on June 27, 1925 to James Lisbon and Charlotte Rovenia (White) Cohen. She was a quiet young woman, the youngest of 12 children, and she was very well cared for. MaDear was the kind of woman who didn't have a lot to say, but when she did speak, everyone would listen. Her family was well-known for their integrity and their influence in the community. They were outstanding members of the Badham Community (located outside of St. George) Jay was the top millwright at the mill. He was so good that his supervisor paid him his salary to keep him on.

MaDear attended South Carolina State College where she had a double concentration in Human Services and Social Work. She often shared the story of riding the train to Orangeburg, S.C. for twentyfive cents. Oh how she loved sharing that story every time she had an opportunity.

During their courtship, He treated her with the respect that she deserved and he respected her parents. He never smoked or drank around her. Even though he went to the juke joint, as they called back then he wouldn't take her.

In 1946, MaDear went on a forty day fast for God to show our grandparents who Daddy really was. After the fast, the Lord revealed to my grandmother that Daddy would love MaDear and take very good care of her, so she and grandfather gave their blessings to MaDear and Daddy to become husband and wife. On July 21st of that same year, they were married, and the legacy of love continues, through their children. She loved Daddy so and believed that he was to be her husband that she fasted, what some. She was so sure that Daddy was the one. "Love is What It Does." MaDear was such an eloquent woman of God. She believed girls should be seen and not heard, and she was very soft spoken. We had to ask her to repeat herself often. As soft spoken as she was, she said what she meant and meant what she said. She could make you cry without raising her voice. Her voice was firm and gentle at the same time. She loved us, and she was always so proud of us and our accomplishments. She was always happy when we said our speeches, sang a song, played an instrument, or performed anything.

Who can find a virtuous woman? for her price is far above rubies. The heart of her husband doth safely trust in her, so that he shall have no need of spoil. She will do him good and not evil all the days of her life. She seeketh wool, and flax, and worketh willingly with her hands. She is like the merchants' ships; she bringeth her food from afar. She riseth also while it is yet night, and giveth meat to her household, and a portion to her maidens. She considereth a field, and buyeth it: with the fruit of her hands she planteth a vineyard. She girdeth her loins with strength, and strengtheneth her arms. She perceiveth that her merchandise is good: her candle goeth not out by night. She layeth her hands to the spindle, and her hands hold the distaff. She stretcheth out her hand to the poor; yea, she reacheth forth her hands to the needy. She is not afraid of the snow for her household: for all her household are clothed with scarlet. She maketh herself coverings of tapestry; her clothing is silk and purple. Her husband is known in the gates, when he sitteth among the elders of the land. She maketh fine linen, and selleth it; and delivereth girdles unto the merchant. Strength and honour are her clothing; and she shall rejoice in time to come. She openeth her mouth with wisdom; and in her tongue is the law of kindness. She looketh well to the ways of her household, and eateth not the bread of idleness. Her children arise up, and call her blessed; her husband also, and he praiseth her. Many daughters have done virtuously, but thou excellest them all.

Proverbs 31:10-20 KJV

MaDear was the woman in Proverbs 31, and her price was far above rubies. The heart of Daddy safely trusted in her without any reservations, and he never regretted it. She did him good and never evil all the days of both their lives. Daddy was spoken of in the gates because of the sacrifices she made to see him be all God called him to be. Our community and surrounding areas knew him as mighty man of God. The high regard of respect that people had for him, was just the will of God.

MaDear knew how to save for each thing without "Robbing Peter to pay Paul." She asked God for wisdom so Daddy could always go to conventions/conferences, stay in nice hotels, and have offerings and spending money. During those times the Shoe Shop was closed for two to three days, that could have been a concern but through God's wisdom she had it all figured out.

She supported Daddy in every area of ministry, and God had no problem reciprocating. She got to enjoy many vacations and trips as a result of honoring Daddy as a husband and as a great man of God. There were so many times when Daddy would have Charlotte and I pack their suitcases, and he would surprise her and take her away. It was nice to have the kind of relationship that you could have her supervisor and the secretary in on the planning so that work was covered. Daddy was a pillar of the community and all the administrative staff, the principal, teachers and employees knew him. He was able to talk with MaDear's supervisor to let him know that he would be traveling and wanted her to be with him.

In the early years of their marriage, MaDear and Daddy unselfishly agreed to live with maternal grandparents by request. MaDear's oldest sister, Wilhelmenia (Big Auntie), moved to Cedarhurst, New York where she worked for many years as a sleep in maid for Mr. Moses Kneiger and his family at 34 Barrett Road to build the house at 509 Gavin St. She finished Apex Beauty School working by day and going to classes at night. Even though she slept in, she had her own room for her days off at 257 Bayview Ave., Far Rockaway, New York. She later moved to 11 School Street, Inwood Long Island, New York.

Momma suffered with high blood pressure. Her blood pressure was always over 200 and she never had a stroke. Her health took a drastic decline in early 1961. Even though MaDear was pregnant, she continued to take care of her mother. Her dedication of love and affection in caring for her mother was something that we always felt as stories were shared about that time.

MaDear and Daddy were able to be there and help out. According to MaDear, before Momma died on September 3, 1961, she asked Daddy to come to her bedside, to thank him for allowing MaDear to be there and to let him know that she appreciated all that he had done for her and Jay. It turned out that the man she wasn't sure about turned out to be one of the best things that ever happened to their family.

Charlotte was born on September 27, 1961, MaDear was very sick following that birth. As a matter of fact, Willerma recalls that Charlotte did not cry when she was born. They kept spanking her. Momma Lelia in her wisdom beyond that of the doctors, sprinkled cold water on her and she released a big cry. She cried a lot until she was five. When Charlotte became tough, she was really tough.

Laughing Moment: I can remember when the Health Department was giving shots for the German Measles at the National Guard Armory, Charlotte and Charlene Govan did not want to take those shots. MaDear had to go down there because, she was screaming, "If I just could see my Momma!" We were thinking, what happened to that tough little girl with so much mouth. She and Charlene were the best friends.

As sick as MaDear was, by faith, she would get pregnant yet again. Charles Leroy Frazier had to come to earth. She would risk her life for the last time on September 27, 1963. We teased them when we got older to say that they mastered it down to a science, two years to the date. A divine assignment that was! This time she was convinced beyond a shadow of a doubt that the doctor was right. Shortly thereafter she and Daddy decided to fix that situation. We figured out why she had to try one more time. Charles was destined to be born into this family without a doubt. God has a way of putting a plan together that we have no clue about. At MaDear's Celebration of Life Services in May 2008, my brother so graciously decided to refer to MaDear and Daddy's relationship as "The Odd Couple." because when they first met people didn't think that they would work out. The life they shared together would not have been possible if they had just given up on knowing they were destined to be together. God knew the plans He had for them; it was so much bigger and better than what others may have thought. They became quite the couple for others to watch and see an example of the love of God. A man who loved God, cherished his wife and loved his family. A woman who loved God, loved and honored her husband and loved her family. When you can set your will to do what pleases God you will get powerful results and your life can be a Godly example for others to follow.

God has a way of putting a plan together that we have no clue about. At MaDear's Celebration of Life Services in May 2008, my brother so graciously decided to refer to MaDear and Daddy's relationship as "The Odd Couple." because when they first met people didn't think that they would work out. The life they shared together would not have been possible if they had just given up on knowing they were destined to be together. God knew the plans He had for them; it was so much bigger and better than what others may have thought. They became quite the couple for others to watch and see an example of the love of God. A man who loved God, cherished his wife and loved his family. A woman who loved God, loved and honored her husband and loved her family. When you can set your will to do what pleases God, you will have powerful results and your life will be a Godly example for others to follow. What an example to many worldwide they were. A classy woman of her time with a meek and humble spirit. MaDear had high moral values and thought that everyone should. She believed little girls should be seen and not heard which meant they shouldn't be loud but have a quiet spirit. She often shared with young married women how to be good wives to their husbands. She believed that a wife should support her husband and stand with him through the good and the times of adversity.

Our parents were committed to the covenant of marriage, they believed that they were responsible for being a good example for their children to follow as they followed Christ. Their love for God was shown through each other, the children and their community. The believed that children are a blessing form the Lord and God was expecting them to bring us up in the fear and admonition of Him.

Her perspective on bringing children up was very clear on these three points:

1. GET TO KNOW YOUR CHILDREN INDIVIDUALLY. Children can't all be disciplined the same way.
2. NEVER COMPARE YOUR CHILDREN TO EACH OTHER. Example: Your sister makes good grades why can't you?
3. NEVER EXPECT OUT YOUR CHILD WHAT YOU KNOW THAT THEY ARE INCAPABLE OF PRODUCING. Know each child's strength and focus on that, never dwell on their weaknesses.

Writing Challenge
What important points have you learned about faith and endurance?

How have you been using faith and endurance to nurture your family?

~~~~~~~30 DAY CHALLENGE~~~~~~~
1. Commit to meditating on the Scripture in this chapter daily.
2. Underline or highlight the strategies in this chapter that you are not already using and commit to using it for 30 days.

Love Is What It Does

One of Daddy's coined sayings is, "Love is what it does." This simply means that when you love, you will do something to show it. Love is an action word. There are so many stories of Daddy's love for God, his family, his church, God's people and people period. Daddy had a very BIG heart he was always willing to help those who were less fortunate than others.

The love that my parents shared was evident to all who knew them and to all who ever came in contact with them. Because of that love and respect it made an impact on others. I can remember them giving college students in our community rides to and from college. They helped people pay their bills at times. They were blessed so they were a blessing to others.

We learned in Ephesians 5:33 that the husband is to love his wife as he loves himself, and the wife must respect her husband. Wives have no problem respecting a man that loves her the way she is supposed to be loved. Our Daddy wanted the very best for his family so he trusted and believed God. MaDear respected Daddy and his decisions and made sure we did the same. She made sure everybody understood he was the "King of 520 North Railroad Avenue."

Her belief was that because Daddy was so respected as a man of God she wanted us to be careful of how we conducted ourselves. She understood that we were children and folly and play was in us but wanted us to know what as expected of us by God not just her and Daddy. She believed that if they were going teach other parents how to train up their children they needed to set the example.

In 1955, Daddy wanted to build a house for his family, but because of the racial prejudice of the times, the white bank loan officers would not give him a loan to do it. The loan officer at the bank said that black people shouldn't have cedar block houses. That did not stop Daddy from doing what was in his heart for his family. He began to buy the materials needed to build his family's new house. He was determined to build this house debt free. In 1959, we moved into our new house, and I was the first child to be born. Don't ever get in the way of a man who loves his family, he will do whatever it takes to give his family the best. "Love is what it does." Though the fight was hard he never gave up on his dream. Some of the wood used was used because when he purchased the new wood some of the pieces rotted before the completion of the home but Mr. Benjamin Warner, owner of Warmer & Sons Funeral Home right next to the house, loaned him the money to buy the materials so he could complete the house.
Willerma remembers taking that loan payment every week to Mr. Warner until it was paid in full.

How to love and forgive people were one the greatest lessons we learned from our parents. They never believed in pitting us against each other or allowing us to remain upset or angry with each other. Teaching us to get along with each other helped us in getting along with others outside our home. If they knew one of us was angry with the other, we had to stand before them to work it out. They believed strongly in not letting the sun go down on our wrath.

Be ye angry, but sin not; let not the sun go down upon your wrath.
Ephesians 4:26 KJV

That was one of the promises they made to each other before they got married so they had to have us walk it out too. To this day, we are still loving and forgiving towards one another. Because of those lessons, we remain very close to each other. It is so important that parents set the example for their children to follow, as God would have it. Unforgiveness can and will destroy good family relationships. The power of forgiveness is to be embraced

How they loved each other, I believe, affected each of us in such a dynamic way. Seeing that love displayed gave us assurance that they would always be together and our family would never be torn apart. We never doubted their love for us. It was just a joy and peace to see how Daddy loved MaDear. We experienced first-hand the kind of love that parents should be expressing every opportunity to be fruitful, multiply and replenish the earth. As a result we lived out God's love.

Writing Challenge
How do you show the God-kind-of-love to your spouse?

How do you show the God-kind-of-love to your spouse?

~~~~~~~~30 Day Challenge~~~~~~~~
1. Commit to meditating on the Scripture in this chapter daily.
2. Underline or highlight the strategies in this chapter that you are not already using and commit to using it for 30 days.

Their Quiver Is Full of Them

Sons are a heritage from the Lord, children a reward from him. Like arrows in the hands of a warrior are sons born in one's youth. Blessed is the man whose quiver is full of them.
Psalm 127:3-5 KJV

For God had blessed Obed-Edom
I Chronicles 26:5 KJV

Children are a blessing from the Lord. We can say that Patrick and Cora Lee Frazier were richly blessed because they gave birth to nine beautiful children. It was a childhood dream of Daddy's to have a large family. So, you can only imagine how proud he was when each of us was born.

Within the first nine months and two days of their marriage, they became the proud parents of a baby girl, Willerma, whose given name was Willie Erma, which they misspelled on her birth certificate and never corrected. Two years later, they gave birth to a baby boy, Patrick, Jr.

While Daddy was sitting on a bar stool, God spoke to him and asked, "Is this the way you want to raise your family?" He knew after God posed the question that he did not want to bring his children up seeing him do what he was doing. He was still drinking and smoking, despite having been diagnosed with Cirrhosis of the liver. Then he was given instructions to go out to Brown's Chapel F.B.H. Church where a revival was in progress. He went and his life was never the same. Daddy got up during the altar call because that was why he was there. God saved, delivered and healed him that night. Daddy fell under the power of God that night, and he always testified that he felt a sharp object like a surgeon's scalpel as if he were having surgery. When he came through he got up feeling as if he never smoked a cigarette in his life and like he had never taken a drink. God miraculously healed and delivered him that night. It was the start of many miracles that would occur in his life.

One of those miracles involved the realization of his childhood dream of raising a large family, Daddy and MaDear had seven more children after his encounter with God in that church. James David was born on May 27, 1951. Susan Patricia was born on August 30, 1953. Bernard was born on May 17, 1955. William Cohen was born on November 24, 1956. Gwendolyn Beverly was born on July 18, 1959. Charlotte Albertha was born on September 27, 1961. Charles Leroy was born on September 27, 1963. Answered prayer, the children are here. This was the beginning of the vision that Daddy had for his family. This vision for the family was that we would all be teachers and preachers of the Gospel of Jesus Christ.

Train up a child in the way he should go and when he is old he will not depart from it.
Proverbs 22:6 KJV

It is the responsibility of parents to instruct children in faith and to teach them the Word of God. In our house, there weren't any lack of instructions in faith or the Word of God. There was never a question about how we would live our lives - **SAVED** was the only option. Our parents believed that we should be saved as early as we could understand what being saved, sanctified and filled with the Holy Ghost meant. There was not a time when we didn't understand that living a life that was set apart for the Master's use was **not** an option. We went to church so much until we got teased about it. Those same teasers wanted to follow or go with us to church often. They would call us "holy rollers".

Daddy was a founder and pastor of a holiness church, Shiloh, which later became Shiloh Fire Baptized Holiness Church of God of The Americas. It started out as a little mission in Mr. Cliff Goodwin's Barber Shop on Gavin Street then later moved to the Byrds Community of St. George. He conducted many revivals at churches throughout the Lowcountry area and throughout South Carolina. Revivals were times not only when people got saved, sanctified and filled with the Holy Ghost but it was also times for those that were spiritually weak to be strengthen to be revived and refreshed. We knew before we left home that MaDear expected us to go down to the altar when the appeal was made at each revival meeting, or she would come to where we were sitting and tell us to go down. During those times, the altar calls were long, and the preachers and altar workers stayed until the people got a breakthrough. There was the clapping of the saint's hands, music (washboards using bent silverware and tambourines, the playing of drums, guitars, piano or organ, singing, shouting and dancing going on at this time. Would you believe some people fell asleep?

And thou shall love the Lord thy God with all thine heart, and with all thy soul, and with all thy might. And these words, which I command thee this day, shall be in thine heart: And thou shalt teach them diligently unto thy children, and shalt talk of them when thou sittest in thine house, and when thou walkest by the way, and when thou liest down, and when thou risest up. And thou shalt bind them for a sign upon thine hand, and they shall be as frontlets between thine eyes. And thou shalt write them upon the posts of thy house and on thy gates.
Deuteronomy 6:5-9 KJV

The Word of God was always before us in either written or spoken form. It was displayed and/or spoken in our home, in our schools, in our community, and everywhere else we went. Devotion, which consisted of family prayer and the reading Scripture, was every morning and every night. Each of us was expected to lead prayer and read Scripture. Sometimes we all had to pray together until the last person was done. Being present at prayer was not an option; it was a command if you were living in our home. Even overnight guests in our house were not exempt. If you were too sick to get out of bed, prayer was around your bed.

Laughing Moment: Our younger brother, Charles tried so hard to be like Daddy that he would pray the same exact prayer Daddy prayed. He imitated everything Daddy did. Daddy always prayed for God to bless the offspring of his body. The very first time it was Charles's time to pray, he asked God to bless the offspring of his body, and we all were stunned. He was too young to have any children. He had no idea what Daddy was saying. He just knew that Daddy prayed it, and he wanted to pray too. We believe it was those prayers that helped shape and mold us into who we are today. We are all serving in the Kingdom of God.

Not forsaking the assembling of ourselves together,
  as the manner of some is; but exhorting one
  another: and so much the more, as ye see the day
  approaching.

Hebrews 10:25 KJV

This scripture definitely operated in our home. We didn't lack in forsaking the assembling of ourselves, or going to church services to be among the saints. James (Jimmy) and Susan went to church to help Daddy in revival for three months straight, including Saturdays and Sundays, without a break. During that time, churches would have two and three week revivals.

Daddy was Rev., Rev. Pat, Pat or Mr. Pat to many. Those who didn't know him through the church met him through the Shoe Shop he owned and operated. It had been known as American Shoe Shop, but he changed the name to Pat's American Shoe Shop when he took over. MaDear became well known in the community because of her role as a social worker for Dorchester County School District I which later became District IV.

All the children knew that if they came over to our house to play, Bible Study was the first thing that was done before playing. They lived their lives in such a manner that everyone knew that God was first in their lives. You would think that would make them not come over, but it was quite the opposite. There are many who have accredited those times at 520 North Railroad Avenue to their being saved today. Several of them are ministers, and some are even pastors. As these children grew older, they went on to accept Jesus as their personal savior. Some accepted Jesus when they would go to church with us. Many of them attended revivals with us and even their parents were happy to have them be with us at church. Not one of those children ever got into serious trouble.

We never heard her talk down about anybody. We never heard her gossiping, and she always corrected us whenever she heard us saying things we heard about people. She was a praying woman, and she talked with the Lord through songs. Susan says she learned to understand MaDear through her songs.

We were not perfect children and there were we disappointed Daddy and MaDear, but they always found it in their hearts to love in spite of. They never compared us to each other. They knew her children. They never expected out of us what they knew we were not capable of producing. Whatever was in you they pushed you to become better at it. They use the same principles for us but allowed us to be individuals.

Everybody in Saint George, South Carolina knew we were one of the Frazier's, so we could hardly do anything that seemed out of character for the preacher's kids. During those times, the preachers and the teachers were well respected. They were held at a higher level of moral living. Preachers and teachers were the closest to seeing God in the flesh.

During those times we understood that if you were allowed to go play at your friend's house, while you were there their parents became your parents. If we misbehaved they were given permission to spank or chastise us and then we received a "whipping" when we got home. It takes a village to raise a child was certainly played out.

Daddy pastored, New Jerusalem F.B.H. Church in the Campbell Thicket section of Ridgeville, SC for 18 years. We spent countless hours at the saints homes. He pastored of New Bethel F.B.H. Church (now known as New Bethel S.O.P.) located in Jedburg, SC, Mt. Zion F.B.H. Church (now known as Greater Mt. Zion Holiness Church in North Charleston) and Mt. Zion F.B.H. in Conway, SC.

Daddy had a radio broadcast on WQIZ, which aired every Sunday morning at 8:00 a.m. That meant that we had to get up and be at the station by 7:30 a.m. for a live broadcast. Sometimes, we taped the broadcast at home, but that didn't happen often. Daddy made an impact over the airwaves as seen through the many letters for prayer requests and praise reports that were received. People were being blessed by the broadcast, and it went on until Daddy started being elevated in ministry as a result of his faithfulness to the Fire Baptized Holiness Church of God of the Americas. He became the Presiding Elder of the Greater Charleston District of the Fire Baptized Holiness Church of God of the Americas.

Daddy had a great healing ministry. He would pray over handkerchiefs and give them out. Many people were healed from cancer, heart conditions, high blood pressure and diabetes. Barren women began bearing children, sons were freed from prison, and husbands were saved. I remember times he would also ask them to place a glass of water near the radio as a point of contact so that even the people he could not physically lay hands on or give a handkerchief to would have something to use to receive the anointing.

We always felt safe around him. There was no doubt in our minds that Daddy would ever let anything or anybody hurt us. He was a loving father and we were so blessed to be his children.

While some children were excited about going to Six Flags, we were excited about Daddy tossing us in the air and catching us before we hit the ground. That was so much better than Six Flags. We loved our lifestyle and especially loved being together. We never felt like our lives were anything but normal and would not have had it any other way.

Our parents loved the unloved and reached the unreached. They lived their lives before us as close to the Bible as they knew, we saw their commitment to the Kingdom. Not once did they complain about having to sacrifice for God or their children. They taught us the Word of God by example-loving with the love of God, nurturing and equipping us for ministry. They taught us values that are still in our families today. They believe that family was important and that you don't get to choose who your family is. They believed you work out any differences because you are family.

Both Daddy and MaDear were family oriented, and we visited family often. Daddy took us over to his mother's house, "Mamma" often, but we didn't go alone. We would always have one of our parents around while we were there, and we would have to come inside and sit with Daddy while our cousins got to stay outside and play. We wondered why. We found out that Daddy didn't want us to hear the conversations the people were having which included some profanity. Uncle Matthew and Aunt Carolyn's house would be one of my favorite houses to visit they always made us feel special. Their marriage was one that was always admired. Their children Bobbie (deceased),Gloria (deceased), Calvin (deceased), Barbara Ann, Peggy, Virgil (deceased), Debra, Nikita and Dwight (now deceased) were such a joy to be around. They always kept us laughing. They also went to church with us quite often.

I remember visiting Lorraine (deceased) and Delores Frazier's house. Their mother Aunt Edith (deceased) was married to our Daddy's brother, Moses (deceased). They also went to church with us sometimes. They were the only family I knew that had four generations all living under one roof.

We would go to Eutawville to visit Aunt Daisy "One" Nelson, she was Daddy's oldest sister. The ride was so much fun. She was so tall and I remember she knew a lot of our family history.

Remembering Uncle George (deceased), He was so tall Uncle Fred (Aunt Helen), Uncle Harry (Aunt Danielle) coming from New York for family visits. It was so exciting to see them.

There were trips to Springtown, SC to visit Uncle Bill, Daddy's brother, and his family. His children, Sylvester, Gloria, Perry, Harold (now deceased) and Harriet (the twins) and Connie (now deceased) We would eat watermelon, took walks down the dirt road, pick plums and watch the people next door work with tobacco. It was all about staying connected to family.

Daddy always took MaDear and us to Sumter, South Carolina to visit her family. We would go to Lane and Gourdin, South Carolina where Jay was from. We took trips to Port Wentworth, Georgia to visit MaDear's brother Uncle Winzer (Sam Gars) who lived there.

Daddy loved taking us on rides in the country, and we always had so much fun. Now people would say we were from the country but we lived in town so a visit to the country was exciting for us. I have several memories of going to the Swagert house. Mrs. Swagert would always come to the car as we were getting out and peep in the station wagon as the last one got out and ask, "Are there any more?" That was her joke for saying my parents had so many children. I remember her having two pretty dogs that they kept inside the house, and I didn't understand why people would have dogs in their houses. I understood dogs to be outside animals. She and Mr. Jim never had any children, and they loved our company.

We took trips to the Deacon Fulton and Sister Celia Winningham's house; they would boil peanuts for us and fix dinner for us. We would spend the day out there; we had lots of fun especially when their grands were visiting from up north.

We would visit Mr. Joe Nathan and Grandma Jane Hudson's house. They were Mrs. Kay Francis McMillian's parents. They were like maternal grandparents to us. We remember smelling the aroma of good food, cakes and pies. They always made us feel like we were their grands by blood.

We would often visit the Callaway family in Hudsontown. As our parents did, they had a bunch of children, doubled the size. The younger children were on age with the younger ones of us. Timothy, Eyvette, Eyvonne, Delmar and Lamar, Jr. Mr. Lamar, Sr, had a little store next door to the house where we could buy candy. At that time we had no idea that Delmar would be married to our sister, Charlotte.

Visiting the saints house was a thrill for, they always loaded us with lots of goodies. Charles always seemed to have the charm; his bag always seemed to be a little bigger. We always use to say he had a special way with the older ladies. He was a little gentleman.

Even though there were nine of us, Daddy always had a special way of making each of us feel as though we were the only child. He knew his children and knew what each of us needed when we need it. I believe he had an anointing on him that he prayed for when it came to his family.

How a man could do all that he did and still managed a loving relationship with his wife and children always amazed us. "Love Is What It Does."

For years we thought we were really millionaires aside from the love and affection. We always wore the latest fashions before they hit the south. We never had SCE&G come turn out lights, Bellsouth never turned our phones off, our water was never turned off and we always had food on the table.

Big Auntie, Wilhelmenia Cohen, spoiled us too. She was MaDear's sister that moved to New York. She never had any children of her own, so, according to her, we were her children. We had the largest doll house with furniture, first walking doll people had ever seen, the newest fashions before others in our area. We always had the best shoes because Daddy knew the importance of taking good care of our feet. They were always the good leather, not necessarily the cutest ones. I remember how those shoes were the toughest to tear up. He only purchased shoes that could be repaired, that meant they had to be leather. His business was known for repairing shoes, and he was the best during his time.

In those days we didn't know of people of color that had ladies to come in and do housework. When mother went to work, Daddy hired someone to come in and do housekeeping two days a week and someone else to iron all the clothes on Thursdays. I remember watching Ms. White iron all of our clothes for the following week. The iron was turned on only that day of the week. MaDear taught the girls how to starch and iron Daddy's handkerchiefs and clergy shirts, but Ms. White handled the rest. Based on those few facts we thought we were millionaires!

Writing Challenge
Which of the strategies for raising children discussed in this chapter would be the most beneficial for your family? How would it change things?

How can you prepare your family for the adoption of the new strategies?

~~~~~~~~30 Day Challenge~~~~~~~~
1. Commit to meditating on the Scripture in this chapter daily.
2. Underline or highlight the strategies in this chapter that you are not already using and commit to using it for 30 days.

Called to Serve

Train up a child in the way he should go: and when he is old, he will not depart from it.
Proverbs 22:6 KJV

We were definitely being groomed and trained to serve as ministers. Our training was done at home, at church, in our community, in our state and nationwide. We participated in many church conferences and functions. Willerma traveled as far as Germany. Training means to enforce, and our parents made sure we understood what we were supposed to be doing. At very early ages, we were given different assignments to fulfill at home and church. There was never a time when we were allowed to say no when asked to participate in any church program or anything to do with church.

On Saturday mornings, the girls went around to clean and help out the elderly ladies in the community. This was considered as a part of ministry. There were times when we wanted to accept money after all the hard work we did. I remember going to clean Mother Flemma Mason Hopkins' house, and she insisted that I take the five dollars she wanted to give me, so I did. When I got home, MaDear asked me if Mother Hopkins gave me any money. I often wondered how she knew, but I knew the Lord told her, and I had to return the money. Since that episode, the elderly ladies knew that money could not be accepted, so they began to bake pies and cakes to show their appreciation. No job was too small or too big because there were enough of us to get the job done.

The girls all took piano lessons, and the boys participated in the band at school. If you didn't sing, you played an instrument: lead guitar, Hawaiian guitar, bass guitar, drums, organ, piano, saxophone, tambourine and trumpet. You name it, and some, or at least one of us could play it. These skills were very useful in ministry. We spent hours at home entertaining our parents singing and playing instruments. Our home was always filled with so much love, joy and peace.

Whenever the saints came to town to take care of business our house was always the house where they came to eat. In those days, you knew you could always find food where there were a lot of children. We always took care of many great men and women of God that came in town. Our parents' bedroom was anointed. We felt like that was the Holy of Holies, where God lived. They had no problem giving up their bedroom so men of God could have a place to rest.
Just to name a few Evangelist Pastor Nelson Eaddy, Prophet Lee, Bishop J. L. McCrakin, Elder F. C. Cantey, Bishop W.E. Fuller, II and Elder and Sister C. P. Tucker and Mother Laura Nichols.

Oh the smell of the kitchen seemed more apparent when they would visit. Cooking was always going on with so many children but those times when the servants of the Most High were there was simply special.

MaDear always loved speeches and literature, so we learned very early on to stand in the front of a crowd. We knew how to pray, how to outline a hymn, how to give welcome addresses, responses, how to outline, write, and teach or preach a sermon, before ever accepting our calling. Of course we all knew we would be called by the Lord. I remember standing in the living room in front of the fireplace reciting speeches for church or school and parts for the operetta. She was a lover of black writers so we learned "The Creation" by James Weldon Johnson before we started school. MaDear could quote and do the dramatic theatrics for it. Some people can only give an account to their first teacher being the one in first grade, but MaDear was our first teacher and the older children taught the younger ones what they learned in school.

MaDear was home with us until our youngest brother turned 4 years old. We learned what we knew about business from our parents because they were business owners in the community. Daddy owned and operated the Shoe Shop for 30 years, and MaDear sold Avon for 40 years while not neglecting ministry or the family.

MaDear went to work as a social worker for Chapter 1 Program for Dorchester County School District One, which is now District Four. Principal A. H. Robinson called and said the district was looking to fill that position and that he thought MaDear would be an excellent choice for the job. The job duties dealt with children taking care of their school and home needs. Daddy told MaDear that she could accept the position if she wanted to but he was not sending her out to work. She accepted and started to work. That made a difference at home. We were used to coming home to her and being there, and now she wasn't. It was exciting to have MaDear working at school, but now we knew we had better not get into any trouble because the news would now get to her fast!

We lived next door to Wamer Funeral home, and there were many times when Daddy was asked to do the eulogy for the deceased at the funeral home and we were the choir and musicians. Some families wanted to pay us for singing, but we were not allowed to accept any money
I remember going into the funeral home one day to view a body and my brother, Bernard thought he would play a joke on us. He went in the back room without us knowing and came out wearing a white sheet. I almost tore the hinges off the screen door of the funeral home. Charlotte and I were so scared. We ran home so fast and locked the doors. That was the day we learned that there wasn't anything to fear

about the dead, it was the living that could make you hurt yourself. Even though our parents though it was funny, Bernard got in trouble for scaring us.

Writing Challenge

If you have children, what strategies and practices are you using to train your children for adulthood? If you don't have children, what strategies and practices did your parents use to train you for adulthood?

What kind of future would you like to see for your children, and how are your current strategies and practices preparing them for it?

~~~~~~~~30 DAY CHALLENGE~~~~~~~~
1. Commit to meditating on this chapter's Key Scripture daily.
2. Underline or highlight the strategies in this chapter that you are not already using and commit to using it for 30 days.

Miracles Do Happen

"And God wrought special miracles by the hands of Paul"

Acts 19:11 KJV

God was doing the Great, the mighty and the miraculous in our parents' life and those that were in contact with them. In 1963, after doctor recommendations to stop having children, MaDear and Daddy found themselves pregnant once again. Shortly after the birth of our younger brother Charles she started hemorrhaging and the doctors were unable to stop it. They were not hopeful that she would survive. Daddy began to pray and the blood stopped.

There were countless women who were barren and Daddy would be instructed by God to pray over a glass of water and have them drink. It would not be long before we would see those women with their babies in their arms. It's so funny now how but, back then I thought something was in the water so I didn't want to drink any water from Daddy. Daddy operated in a prophetic anointing that would have others in awe of the gift. Whatever he prophesied came to pass. People reverence God and the anointing that he operated in.

Testimony - Sister Mary Jane Daniels *(Aunt of Pastor Gralin Hampton)*

I remember almost like it was yesterday. Sister Mary Jane Daniels passed out on the front row during a Sunday morning service. This happened at Shiloh Fire Baptized Holiness Church of God of the Americas in Byrds, SC. Unknown to me and many others at the time she was not slain in the spirit, she was dead. All of her body fluids had release from her body. The process that takes place at death occurred. Daddy came down from the pulpit and laid hands on her as the saints gathered around. I remember her lifeless body slowly returning among the living. It was an experience I never forgot. I was about ten or eleven years old at the time. Afterwards she gave her testimony that we were there this time but the next time it happens, no one would be around. I understood later she was ready and wanted to go.

The story of Lazarus became more real to me. I had heard it preached so many times and I had read it the Bible before, but that day brought revelation to me of what took place when Jesus raised Lazarus from the dead. I knew then that this was not just something Jesus could do or something that was a thing of the past. It became real to me that Daddy and the saints had the power within them to raise the dead. After seeing Sis Daniel raised from the dead, I wanted him to do that for everybody that died. I thought, oh wow, we never have to feel the hurt and pain of death again. People would die and Daddy could pray and they would come back to life. I was so excited about my new found revelation. I asked Daddy those questions and his response was, "Death is an appointment that we all have to make, He went on to say it was already appointed for man to die. He told me thatthere was a time to live and a time to die. He said to me that we could not live in eternity with our natural bodies so death has to take place, so we can live again.

Miracles Can Happen with Automobiles Too.

We had a car that would not go in reverse due to transmission problems. Daddy tried calling the mechanic and was unsuccessful in doing so. The Spirit of the Lord spoke to him and told him to go outside and lay hands on the hood. Well Daddy obeyed the voice of God. Them He told him to get in and put the car in reverse, well the car went in reverse. A few days later the mechanic contacted Daddy about the car and when Daddy told him it was working, he couldn't believe it. He knew there was a serious problem with the car's transmission. The car did not have anymore problems with the transmission and was still working when Daddy traded it in on another car years later. God created the materials used to make the car and gave man the knowledge and ability to design and make it, why wouldn't he have the power to repair it without a mechanic.

In 1979, Daddy became very ill and many tests were preformed to determine the problem. Doctors discovered that he had type II diabetes. If he didn't get control of it fast, it would eventually kill him. After much research and study, a change in his diet was done and it wasn't long before he was feeling better and did not go on insulin at that time. He often said if someone had told him how important it was to stay away from certain foods, he would have done a better job of caring for his body. Daddy enjoyed high seasoned foods and lots of pork.

In 1987, The diabetes became life threatening. He started having problems with poor blood circulation in his big toe. Doctors tried to get it under control, but it just seemed to not work. In June of that same year, Daddy was admitted into Medical University of South Carolina in an executive suite.

There he would be for the next three months. This was a faith walk for our family and something that was new to us. What I remember the most was my parents unwavering faith that his sickness would not result in death. He shall not die but live; to declare the works of the Lord. Gradually, they began amputations, starting with toe, and then another toe, and then his entire foot. Daddy never wimped out on us, he was tough through it all. He encouraged us through this ordeal by his strength of character.

When month three arrived, the doctors called the family together and told us that they had to amputate Daddy's left/right leg from just below his knee down. It was hard for us to take, but the one thing we were not willing to do was give up on him. In September of 1987, Daddy was able to come home. His life as he knew it before had changed physically, but his spirit was even stronger. There were ramps built to accommodate the wheel chair he now needed. Bars were put in place to assist in the bathroom.

In 1987, at the age of 66, Daddy experienced yet another test of faith. Daddy was diagnosed with melanoma, a rare skin cancer that was not popular among the black race at that time. The doctors were in disbelief. How could this black man have developed this disease? It baffled the medical team at the Veteran's Hospital. I remember so many doctors in and out the room when the results came back. Before they could share that with us they had to make sure the results were correct. He was given six months to live.

Every time he showed up for an appointment after that, they were shocked. He would speak in tongues, and they wanted to know that language that he spoke. During his visits, he would pray for patients and even some of the doctors. He gained such a respect for his love and belief in God until he was trusted to give advice on matters. For the next six years, Daddy went to his appointments. In 1997, his other leg was amputated because the melanoma had spread from the bottom of his foot up his leg. The man they expected to be dead in six months was still alive preaching the Gospel with more fire and passion then ever before. This was a testimony of his faith in the God he served.

In January 2004, Daddy was sent him home from an appointment to die within two weeks because the cancer had spread to his brain. Daddy didn't give up, and he did out lived his expected time in hospice. The gentleman that they sent to be his nurse was so impressed with Daddy until he got attached to him and ended up quitting his job because he couldn't take knowing that this great man would one day die. He asked if he could bring his wife and children to meet him, and he did.

We watched our mother love out the "in sickness and in health" part of her wedding vows. He was so concerned about MaDear because she started losing weight taking care of him, and he never wanted to be a burden to her or us. We assured him that he wasn't and could never be.

Daddy died on August 1, 2004, seventeen years after being diagnosed with melanoma without chemotherapy, which was quite unusual. I remember how brave he was about facing death. He was not fearful of what was about to take place. He welcomed the idea of going to be with the Lord. In fact, he had chosen the day. The day he died we buried his oldest sister and we believe that he wanted to go while the out of town relatives were here and would not have to come back. It was just one of his ways he often thought of others. On many occasions Daddy talked about living to the ripe age of one hundred but he changed his mind, he grew tired.

I never imagined living on this earth without my parents. As a child, just the very thought of not being able to see or talk with them was very frightening to me. It really scared me when one of the saints would pass away, and I prayed to the Lord to keep my parents alive forever Now that they both have passed away, the faith in God and their display of love and family helps us to deal with life's issues.

MaDear did well for the first two years but it became evident that she was missing him I had the opportunity to take care of her on a daily basis for the last ten months of her life. During this time she talked about Daddy so much you could feel her hurt aching for him. In February 2008 she told me that she talked with Daddy and he was in bed lying next to her. I asked her why was he there he was gone on to be with the Lord. She would just smile.

On March 23, 2008 Easter Sunday she made a special request of Eugene and I. She asked that we come and drive her to the eight o'clock service at Willerma's church. We agreed to do so and since all of our children were home for the holiday they went with us. After that service she said she wanted to go to Charles' church for the eleven o'clock service. At the time she was on oxygen and we thought it would be depleted before returning home. She was so adamant about being there. We tried to take her home, even when we pulled up in the yard she refused to get out of the van. She told us we didn't have anything to do and we could take her. Well needless to say she got her wish. We went and she enjoyed herself thoroughly. Dinner was served after the services and we left the church around 5:00 p.m. While on the way to her house she asked Eugene to ride through the town and she began to reminisce about the town, things that happened there, what building had changed and the people who had already died. Upon arriving home we discovered that her oxygen was never turned on and the amazing thing was she was not affected by it. On previous occasions when it ran out she would become very weak. We were quite alarmed by that discovery.

On the following Monday, March 24, when I went to her house to care for her while Willerma went to work when I got there Willerma was still there she planned to go in late. MaDear was eating breakfast and finished up the last fork full when she told me she wanted to lay down. She asked me to get her walker and I did. As usual I would turn and sit on the walker until she got up so it would not tilt. When I would do this she would comment that I had a lot of "rumpus" (my behind) to sit on back there. This time she didn't say anything so that was strange so when I turned around her head and chin was dropped to her chest. I called her name and she didn't respond so I called out to Willerma and told her to come and hold her up while I call 911. Of course when Willerma saw she started screaming and I told her to pray there wasn't time for that. I placed the call and could not find the cordless phone so my view was not clear for keeping an eye on MaDear, The dispatcher was asking questions that I had to put the phone down to run and see. All the ambulances were out on call, the fire truck was the only vehicle they could sent at that time.

We began to pray and command Cora Lee Frazier's spirit man to rise up, "you will not die but live to declare the works of the Lord. Live Cora Lee LIVE, IN JESUS NAME!!!" I had witnessed the dead coming back to life before this was not new. Fear never entered my heart. We called her name again and she came through and responded and said "Why did you all call EMS?" You all are going to have to pay those hospital bills when I go. She was not interested in staying here. When the fire truck got there she was sitting up.

After checking her vital signs that said they needed to take her to the hospital. She was transported to MUSC. Willerma rode in the ambulance with her. When they left and I sat down I felt fear like I had never experienced. I thought about what just happened. MaDear had left us and I started to think about the day before and the events that had transpired. She was letting us know but we didn't get it. When she left that day she never came back home. She would spend the next 8 weeks between the hospital and a rehabilitation facility. During this time she was experiencing constant episodes of her oxygen level dropping which would cause her to black out.

She was transported to Summerville Medical where she would remain until she was better. After 3 weeks she became weak in her legs and could not walk due to just lying in bed so then she had to receive physical therapy to regain her muscle strength. There was an incident when her spirit left her body and I showed up, she wasn't in her room. They had taken her to run some test. When I stepped out of the room and went down the hall, they were taking her to ICU. The doctors and nurses were crying and I asked what the problem was. I was informed that her hemoglobin had dropped from twelve to three. When I looked at her she was lifeless and not talking. I called her and she didn't answer. Without even thinking I laid my hands on her chest and said Cora Lee Frazier you will live and not die, IN THE NAME OF JESUS!!! And I began to speak in others tongues and the next time I called her name she said, "Hi baby". She told me that we would be left to pay these hospital bills. She stayed in ICU for 3 days, but she was still alive with us and talking. When she got a little stronger she was sent to a nursing rehabilitation facility where she was for about one week than had to return to the hospital from an infection.

While at that facility, on April 18, before I went to feed her breakfast I asked God to let me know what

MaDear wanted as far as living was concerned. When I got there and she took the last spoon full of food and drank her juice she began to talk. She said she wanted to thank me for taking such good care of her, she was so thankful for all that her children had done for her. She made this statement, "If I ever had any doubt in my mind about how much my children loved me. It was all cleared up. You all really love your momma."

She went on to say she thank God for having a wonderful husband who was a great father. She bragged about how spoil he had her and we could never fill his shoes. She expressed her appreciation for the life God allowed her to live, places she had been and the people she had met. She talked about seeing Jesus and being in the presence of God. She talked about how much she missed our Daddy and wanted to go where he was. Her mind was fixed and there was no talking her out of it so I didn't try. She then began to tell me how she wanted her funeral.
Then she told me she wanted me to sing the song she always loved to hear me sing, "I'm Going Up Yonder".

She told me that she wanted Jimmy to do her eulogy because she believed he was strong enough to. Patrick had done Daddy's and Charles did his wake. She expressed that she wanted her children and grandchildren to be the choir. She told me to make sure that we support and help Patrick, who was taking on a great responsibility as presiding bishop of the Fire Baptized Holiness Church of God of the Americas. She said she would not be here for Tina's wedding, May 30 or Delmeria baby's birth in October. I asked her would she be here for Jeffrey's graduation which was June 7, she said no. Then I asked if she would be here for her birthday, June 27 she wasn't sure. She stated if she wasn't she still wanted a birthday party. This great woman of God even in longing to leave earth still was concerned about her family. She had a way of knowing what we needed when we didn't.

She told me to call Jimmy and tell him to come when he got off work. She talked for about two hours and then I told her I had to go to the car. When I got in the van I didn't know I could cry so much. I called Eugene and he got there so fast. I sent a text message out to my siblings letting them know that MaDear was ready to leave us. I didn't know how soon but they needed to come.

MaDear would return back Summerville Medical to be treated for the infection. On April 24 she was sent to another rehabilitation facility. It was there that she received physical therapy and improved with her walking. Around the end of April she requested that we all come to Charlotte's house to have Mother's Day dinner with her. That was a request that she had never made. Most of my siblings are pastors and she knew how important it is for pastors to be at their churches. Plans were made to make it happen. She was scheduled to go home on May 16 and we were excited about that.

The following accounts were experienced by me because I spent days with Ma Dear because I was not working and all of my siblings were working full time. They were very supportive and MaDear always believed if you had a job, keep attendance as perfect as you could. They all give of their time when they could, they visited her after work and on weekends while she was in the hospital and at rehab.

During the week of May 6, 2008 I had picked up a virus and did not want to put the facility at risk so I stayed away and checked on her everyday. I had already purchased two cards for her and was prompted to mail one card. I felt strange and started not to but felt pushed to go to the mailbox on May 8 then on May 10, at about 9:30 p.m. I felt so impressed to go to see her. When I got there she was sleeping, after about ten minutes I woke her up. When she looked at me her words were, I knew you were coming. She thanked me for the beautiful card I sent her. She made me promise that everyone would be at Delmar and Charlotte's house the next day in Summerville, SC. I said to her she would be there too and she acted as if I didn't say that. She was so happy about all the flowers and beautiful cards that she received that day. We talked a bit and she told me not to come in the morning and I told her I would be there to help her with breakfast. That was a little odd for her to say that. I said goodnight and left out the building but when I got in the car it was an hour before I could drive off.

On Sunday, May 11, I overslept and jumped up hit the shower to go see her. By the time I got dressed the phone rang and I said, "Oh no MaDear not on Mother's Day!" Then told Eugene MaDear has left us. I knew it before I answered the phone. The lady asked if we could come now. When we got there the nurses looked so sad then we were asked to go in the conference room. Jimmy and Lavern were waiting in the conference room. They faces told the story. I couldn't cry, I felt strength like I felt when Daddy passed.

When they took us in the room the song "I'm Free" just came out of my spirit and we sang it. MaDear was at peace and we knew she was happy. Once again she was taking care of us. She picked that morning to leave and she knew we needed to be together. It was just so like her to set us up for our good. All of the children and grandchildren were under one roof that day celebrating Mother's Day honoring a woman who was the epitome of strength.

That day was joyful day of fun and laughter. We reminsecne about how MaDear always knew that we would need each other on this day. She lived such a life before God and others that she picked the day she would leave this earth. What an exceptional woman.

People came from far and near to celebrate the life of a woman who was mother of nine but MaDear to many. She touched the lives of so many people young and old alike. It was not strange for young people sit at her feet to get wisdom on life events. She didn't like being around people her age, she said they complained too much about aches and pain in their bodies. It wasn't strange for her and Daddy to spend time with people 10-20 years younger.

Will parents ever get everything right? Probably not, but I hope this book has encouraged parents to do all that is in their power to have a vision for your family.

Where there is no vision, the people perish...

Proverbs 29:18a

Do everything within your power to live a life before your children that you would be proud for them to immolate. There are many methods but the message remains the same: bring your children up in the fear and adoration of the Lord.

Will they always do everything right? No way! But when you have done your part, they will come back to the values you instilled in them. It is important as Christians that our children are raised according to the Word of God. It takes discipline and structure to bring your children up working in ministry because of the pressures they have to want to be like other kids, but it can be done.

And God Blessed Them

Psalm 128, I believe can be used to describe our family.

Blessed is every one that feareth the LORD; that walketh in his ways. For thou shalt eat the labour of thine hands: happy shalt thou be, and it shall be well with thee.Thy wife shall be as a fruitful vine by the sides of thine house: thy children like olive plants round about thy table. Behold, that thus shall the man be blessed that feareth the LORD. The LORD shall bless thee out of Zion: and thou shalt see the good of Jerusalem all the days of thy life. Yea, thou shalt see thy children's children, and peace upon Israel.

Psalm 128:1-6 KJV

A good father fears God and walks in His ways. He chooses the right path for himself and his family. The right path could not have been easy for Daddy but because he feared God and wanted the best life for his family he made the choice to do so. Remember God presented him with the question, "Is this how you want to raise your family"? as he was sitting on that baar stool. He made the decision to train up his children in the way we should go and even when we are old we will not depart from it *(Proverbs 22:6)* Daddy knew that he had to bring us up in the discipline and the instruction of the Lord and that he could not provoke us to anger *(Ephesians 6:4)* If we go back up to *Psalm 127:3-4* it clearly tells us that children are a blessing from the Lord. *"Behold, children are a heritage from the Lord, the fruit of the womb a reward. Like arrows in the hand of a warrior are the children of one's youth.*

For thou shall eat the labor of thine hands: Daddy always planted a garden that provided fresh vegetables for our family. He was a businessman that provided for his family at all times. There was never a time that we felt we were not well taken care of.

The Contemporary English Version says, *The Lord will bless you if you respect Him and obey His laws. Your fields will produce, and you will be happy and all sill go well. Your wife will be as fruitful as a grapevine, and just as an olive tree is rich with olives, your home will be rich with healthy children. That is how the Lord will bless everyone who respects Him. I pray that the Lord will bless you from Zion and let Jerusalem prosper as long as you live. May you live long enough to see your grandchildren. Let's pray for peace in Israel!*

Psalm 128:1-6

Thank God for our parents pulling out of us what they thought we need to, to do what God had purposed for each of us to. They were so happy to see all of us operating in our gifts and displaying our talents. It gave them such joy to see that fruit of their labor was not in vain. Daddy wanted to bring up preachers, so God blessed him and granted him his request. He made the decision "As for me and my house, we are going to serve the Lord".

Today, all of their children are saved, sanctified, and filled with the Holy Ghost with the evidence of speaking in other tongues. There are eight preachers by birth, six by marriage and one ordained deacon.

As a result of our parents' prayers, we have one Senior Bishop, two presiding elder, four pastors, two ministers, and one first lady who is in denial. Charlotte holds to her truth that she was called to be a pastor's wife. The second and third generation has three ministers and counting.

It is my sincere hope that you have enjoyed this book. It is quite obvious that the way they did it had such an impact on us that we could not deny or run far away from what we were called to do.

I trust that you will walk away knowing that God has a plan for every family and that you desire find out that specific plan for your family.
God's plan for the family is simple, yet we complicate it by bringing our own ideas into the plan. Husbands love your wives.

Wives, honor your husbands. Children, obey your parents. Parents, bring your children up in the fear and admiration of the Lord. There are individual assignments for every family member.

If you are all about ministry, train your children to be just that too. Your children will love what you love when you start them early. Don't make excuses as to why you can't fit family prayer into your schedule. Children need to see and hear your prayers. Your spouses need to hear what you are praying. The power of agreement is at work when everybody is on one accord.

There are times when we missed the mark but the key is to get back on track and keep moving forward.

I do believe that because of our upbringing that was filled with a lot of praying together and our parents teaching us the power of forgiveness that we all remain very close today. We look forward to spending time with each other and our families. Our children even have close relationships with each another because of the example they saw. They too experienced prayer with their grandparents.

Writing Challenge:

After reading this chapter, what are some major changes you will make as husband/wife, father/mother or has someone who is considering being one of the above?

How to Get From Where You Are

"And the Lord answered me, and said, Write the vision, and make it plain upon the tables, that he may run that readeth it." Habakkuk 2:2

There should be specific family times established early on.

Find a church that supports the family and family activities. The pastor should value family relationships as they relate to the Word of God.

Marriage should be important. If you of thinking of getting married decide now with your future spouse how will prayer be handled and how you will introduce your children to prayer. Make prayer a priority in your family's life.

Prayer is vital to your life so don't take it likely. We make schedules and to do list on our jobs and most of us never write the vision for prayer for us and our families. If prayer is something you are not accustomed to doing it will take practice. Start with a prayer plan.

If this is going required of your children to pray, they should hear and see you prayer. You wouldn't want a teacher to through a responsibility at your children without first instructions and demonstration of it.
Include on your calendar a time to pray with your children/family.

Family prayer is very important for all.

> *"For where two or three are gathered together in my name, there am I in the midst of them."*
>
> Matthew 18:20 KJV

It is important that each family member have their own private time of prayer.

Prayer should be done as a couple; this is where the power of agreement comes in.

> *"Again I say unto you, That if two of you shall agree on earth as touching any thing that they shall as, it shall be done for them of my Father which is in heaven."*
>
> Matthew 18:19 KJV

Something powerful happens when a husband and wife take the time out to pray together. II have countless testimonies of seeing what happens when a family comes together in prayer.

Prayer and scripture reading should be done with your children. Small children should start out with short prayers that first give thanks to God. Scriptures should be used so they learn early on to pray the Word of God.

Use Children Bible stories as a start so they can relate to the Bible.

Choose prayer times that fit your family's schedule keeping in mind that it may take some sacrifice on making it happen.

Plan family meetings. Determine how often and have an agenda. Set family goals and do follow-ups. Discuss where you are and what changes need to be made, be honest.

Dinner or Supper can be a good time to find out what is happening in your children's lives.

    Remember, *Where there is no vision, the people perish... Proverbs 29:18a*

Make an Impact Write Now:

Write the vision for your family and share it with family members. Set realistic goals and establish some short term goals the are obtainable.

The following pages contain prayers that maybe used to get you started. Remember that if we have any anger, bitterness, resentment, pride, irritation, selfishness or unforgiveness in our hearts, our prayers will not be answered. When you pray make sure your heart is right.

"If I regard iniquity in my heart, the Lord will not hear"
Psalm 66:18

"Be anxious for nothing; but in everything by prayer and supplication with thanksgiving let your requests be made known unto God."
Philippians 4:6 KJV

Enter into His gates with thanksgiving, and into His courts with praise. Be thankful to Him, and bless His name.
Psalm 100:4 KJV

"Husbands, likewise, dwell with them with understanding, giving honor to the wife, as to the weaker vessel, and as being heirs together of the grace of life, that your prayers may not be hindered"
I Peter 3:7 KJV

Prayer for Husbands

Father, in the name of Jesus, help me to be the husband that loves his wife as Christ loves the church. Help me to always honor and respect her as your daughter and my queen. In times when I feel any hurt, disappointment, anger or frustration, help me to quickly release it so that my prayers are not hindered.

Father, I submit my will to you so you can do the leading so I don't go my own way. Help me to die to the flesh daily in my marital relationship. Not my will but your will be done.

Father I thank you for my wife. Help me to be patient, loving and kind and always forgiving towards her. Help me to be the husband that my wife needs. Help me to always pray for her, to always compliment her not criticize, help me to encourage her in achieving her plans and goals.

Help me to always find sexual fulfillment in our marriage bed for you said marriage is honorable, above all and the bed is undefiled.

Father I thank you that our marriage will be the Godly example that our children and others need to see. Let our sons see a Godly man as husband so that it leaves such an impression that they want to be a husband like their father. Let our daughters see a husband that they would desire for themselves when that time comes.

Prayer for Wives

Father, in the name of Jesus, help me to be the wife that always loves, honors and respects her husband. Help me to never hold on to past hurts or mistakes. It is my desire to be better as a better listener, friend, lover and confidante. You have said in your word that I should be kind to him, tenderhearted, forgiving even as God in Christ forgave me.

Father I submit my will to you for you can do the leading so I don't do my own way. Help me to die to the flesh daily in this martial relationship. Not my will but your will be done.

Father I thank you for my husband. Help me to always be patient, loving, kind and forgiving towards him. Help me to be the husband that my husband needs. Help me to always pray for him, to always compliment him not criticize, help me to encourage him in achieving his plans and goals.

Help me to always find sexual fulfillment in our marriage bed for you said marriage is honorable, above all and the bed is undefiled.

Father I thank you that our marriage will be the Godly example that our children and others need to see. Let our daughters see a Godly woman as wife so that it leaves such an impression that they want to be a wife like their mother. Let our sons see a wife that they would desire for themselves when that time comes.

Prayers for Parents

Father, in the name of Jesus, we come to you believing that you have entrusted our children to us to nurture and care for them. We thank you for giving us the knowledge in your word how we are to go about doing this. Help us to always seek your counsel through successful others when necessary.

Father, we thank you for our children because they are a gift from you. Help us to be loving and kind to them, always loving and forgiving as you forgive us. We thank you that we will always be able to provide for their natural needs and show them how to get from you the spiritual they need.

Father we thank you that you will always put others in their lives that are critical for their assignment in life. Help us to bring them up in the nurture and admonition of you. Help us to show them by example how to live a life set apart for your use.

Father, we thank you for wisdom, knowledge and understanding on making the right choice when disciplining each of them so we don't destroy their spirit.

Prayer for Your Children

Dear Father, Thank you for this day you have made and I am happy to rejoice in it. Thank you for your Son Jesus who gave his life that I might be free. Thank you for His blood that makes me clean from all my sins. I love you because you love me.

Please fill me with your spirit today as I go along my way. Lord bless my family, they are special to me. Give you angels charge over us to keep in all our ways. Help me to be mindful of others who may not know you. Help me to let my light so shine that my friends will want to get to know you. Bless my principle, my teachers, my bus driver and all the staff workers at my school. Help them to be patient and kind to all the students.

Lord I will be careful in everything I say or do. I want to make you happy and please you all the days of my life. Thank you for blessing me and keeping me.

Prayer for Your Pastor, Wife and his Family

Father, we thank you for a God Fearing First Family. We thank you for a pastor after you heart, full of love and the compassion of Christ. We thank you for his prayer and study time that will not be interrupted with distractions. We thank you that he is focused and alert at all times. We thank you that you put others around him that have his spirit.

Father we thank you for a man of God who loves you and loves his wife. We thank you for a pastor who is the head of his house and lives before us your example of the relationship of Christ and the church. Thank you for a pastor who instructs his children in Your Word. Thank you Father for his wife, who is an example of a meek and quiet spirit who supports her husband in ministry.

Father we thank you that the First Family is shield and protected from attacks of the enemy. We pray that they will not get weary in well doing. Lord heal them from any hurt that has been caused by ministry so that they can move forward and continue to feed you people with the Word we need.

Prayer for the President and Vice President and their Families

Father we thank you for our President, Vice President and their families. We thank you for leading them in the way you desire for the United States of America to move forward. We thank you that they will always seek your counsel from those you have appointed and assigned to them. Father we thank you that they will come to know you as Lord of their lives. We thank you that they will become filled the Holy Spirit with the evidence of speaking in other tongues as the spirit gives utterance. We thank you that they seek you early in the morning before in day is started.

Father we thank you for guiding them and helping to see your heart concerning Israel. We thank you Father for giving them revelation on the importance of Israel's land to them. Help them to quickly repent for entering into any agreements that go against your will.

Father help them to stand up for what you believe in and not compromise and make decisions against what this nation is suppose to represent.. Remind them daily that they are accountable to You God FIRST and that they need to be led by your voice and not the voice of others. Help them to hate what you hate and love what you love. IN JESUS NAME!!!

Prayer for Those Who Serve and Protect Us

Father we thank you for all those who serve and protect us in our communities and our country. We thank you for police officers, our firefighters, our military and armed forces. Thank you because they have chosen to be the peacemakers and conquerors. We thank you for their families who also make the sacrifice that we sometimes take for granted.

We pray they call upon the name of the Lord and be saved. We plead the Blood of Jesus over each and every one of them and their families. Thank you for Divine strategies to defeat our enemies.

Give your angels charge over them to keep and protect them and bring them back safe to their families. IN JESUS NAME!!!!

Daily Scripture Readings

The fruit of the Spiritit is love, joy, peace, longsuffering, kindness, goodness, faithfulness, gentleness, self-control. Against such there is no law. Galatians 5:22-23 KJV

You are a chose generation, a royal priesthood, a holy nation, His own special people, that you may proclaim the praises of Him who called you out of darkness into His marvelous light. I Peter 1:10

If any of you lacks wisdom, let him ask of God, who gives to all liberally and without reproach, and it will be given to him. James 1:5

I will give you the keys of the kingdom of heaven, and whatever you bind on earth will be bound in heaven, and whatever you loose on earth will be loosed in heaven. Matthew 16:19

The Lord shall preserve your going out and your coming in from this time forth, and even forevermore. Psalm 121:8

There is no fear in love; but perfect love casts out fear, because fear involves torment. But he who fears has not been made perfect in love. I John 4:18

Pleasant words are like honeycomb, sweetness to the soul and health to the bones. Proverbs 16:24

He will keep him in perfect peace, whose mind is stayed on Him, because he trusts in Him. Isaiah 26:3

Obey those who rule over you, and be submissive, for they watch out for your souls, as those who must give account. Let them do so with joy and not with grief, for that would unprofitable for you. Hebrews 13:17

Put off, concerning your former conduct, the old man which grows corrupt according to the deceitful lusts, and be renewed in spirit of your mind, and ...put on the new man which was created according to God, in true righteousness and holiness. Ephesians 4:22-24

Do not be conformed to this world, but be transformed by the renewing of your mind, that you may prove what is that good and acceptable and perfect will of God. Romans 12:2

If we walk in the light as He is in the light, we have fellowship with one another. I John 1:7

Though we walk in the flesh, we do not war according to the flesh. For the weapons of our warfare are not carnal but mighty in God for the pulling down strongholds, casting down arguments and every high thing that exalts itself against the knowledge of God, bringing every thought into captivity to the obedience of Christ.
II Corinthians 10:3-5

For what profit is it to a man if he gains the whole world, and loses his own soul? Or what will a man give in exchange for his soul?
Matthew 16:26

Through wisdom a house is built, and by understanding it is established; by knowledge the rooms are filled with all precious and pleasant riches.
Proverbs 24: 3-4

Be kind to one another, tenderhearted, forgiving one another, even as God in Christ forgave you.
Ephesians 4:32

The Shoe Shop on Railroad Avenue

Special Thanks to Some Very Special People

To **Eugene**, my wonderful loving husband who has encouraged me throughout writing this book. Thank you for the life lessons that caused me to walkout what I know, that is to walk in love and forgiveness even when I didn't know I could. Thank you for all your encouragement and support.

To my children, **Terrance**, **Trenise** and **Jeffrey**, thank you all for your encouragement, love and support. I am truly blessed to be your mother.

To my Pastor, **Dr. Johnathan Briggs**, a very special thanks for pulling out of me what needed to be said to help others. I am so glad I was in included in God's plan for your life. I honor you as my father in the faith and my pastor. Thanks to **Lady Subrena Briggs** for trusting your husband to be who he is in the Body of Christ.

To my siblings, Intercessor **Willerma** Frazier-Riley (Minister Floyd), Bishop **Patrick** (Minister Lady Sharon) Frazier, Jr., Pastor **James** (Minister Lady Laverne) Frazier, Pastor **Susan** P. (Pastor Andrew) Wilson, Pastor **Bernard** Frazier, Presiding Elder **William** C. (Minister Lady Kathy L.) Frazier, Lady **Charlotte** Callaway (Pastor Delmar) Callaway, Presiding Elder **Charles** (Minister Lady Sylvia) Frazier, Mrs. Barbara A. Kelly (Thad), Ms. Rosa Davis, Ms. Bobbie Jean Davis, Ms. Cleve Mack, Ms.

Judy Cusack, Ms. Gracie Hill, **Attorney Carl Grant**, Ms. Patricia Parker and Ms. Erica Russell, thank you for keeping the lessons of loving family alive in your children. I am so happy to be a part of this wonderful loving family. We are doing what we have been trained to do. You all are "Sweeter than Sugar, You are Honey."

To all my nieces, Yolanda Stallworth, Minister Irma (Minister Travis) Gomillion , Minister Tera (Corey) Moses, Dr. Anita M. (Charles) Rawls, Lady Coren (Pastor Paul) Burch, Minister Gratina "Tina" (Minister Corey) Taylor, Patrice Frazier, Omega S. Frazier, Delmeria (Sean) Biggs and Shawana Frazier, Nkechi Frazier, Charlotte "Frosty" Callaway, Victoria "Vicky" Callaway and Precious Callaway and Tanika "Nek" Smith for all you help with formatting and long hours. And to my anointed nephews, Jamil Rivers Frazier, James L. Frazier, Lavoris (Monique) Frazier, William Frazier, II.

To Aunt Ruth (McBride), thank you for all your encouragement, your sweet hugs and the way you say, I love you from your heart. You are a jewel and it is so good to know that you are there when we need you.

To Uncle Fred (Aunt Helen) Frazier, thank you for all your love and support always.

To Uncle Harry (Aunt Danielle) Frazier, who shows up at every invite because he truly loves being with his family. Thank you for being there for us.

To Apostle Allen (Lady Janice) Simmons, thank you for all your support you have given to our family and continue to. Our parents were so very proud to call you their son. You are our "Big Brother."

To Bishop Theotis (Elder Vernethia) White who have always respected our parents as their own. Thank you for your encouragement throughout the years to our family and continue to this day.

Thanks to Apostle Frederick K.C. Price for his teaching on marriage. He was the first television minister that I heard teaching on marriage the way I saw it through my parents and the way I thought it should be. He was a mentor from afar.

To Mrs. Catherine "Ms. Cat" Rolack, who was very instrumental in us learning some important facts about this love story and about our parents. She and her late husband, Mr. Sylvester (now deceased) were the sports parents of the neighborhood. Thank you for being a good neighbor to us. My brothers enjoyed many good times at your house. Thank you for your love and support.

To Pastor Richard and Sister Rosa Lee Thompson, Minister Mary P. Reed, Minister Mary Britt and their families for all their love and support as members of Shiloh F.B.H. Church. Thank you for believing in the vision God gave Daddy.

To Deacon Edgar and Sister Emma Green who always welcomed us in their home and showed us such love and respect. We became their family for life.

To Mother Estelle Hilton (who has passed away before this new edition was printed) and the late Deacon Willie Hilton, thank you for your continued support. Thank you for taking care of our family when Daddy was your pastor. Long life God has satisfied you with long life. We ate many dinners in your home.

To Pastor Carl (who is now deceased) and Lady Joetta Bellinger, thank you for loving and respecting our parents the way you did. MaDear always made it known to us that Elder Carl was "her son." To Deacon George Melvin (who is now deceased) and Sister Annabelle Wright, who my parents loved dearly. MaDear always said Deacon Melvin Wright was her deacon.

To Brother David and Inez "Doll" Shuler, thanks for always loving and supporting our family.

To Deacon Moses Jr. and Geraldine Simmons, who always supported our parents and their ministry.

To the late Wilhelmenia "Big Auntie"Cohen (MaDear's oldest sister), thank you for making it possible for us to live like the rich and famous in our fashion. Thank you for supporting us to be the best that we could be.

To the late Mr. Paul Hutto, our father's friend during a time when it was not a norm for this type of friendship because of racial barriers. He saw a great man in my father in spite of the color of his skin.

To the late Miss Agalee Salley (Nana) who loved Daddy so much and respected him so much, she knew God would use him to speak a word in her situation.

To Pastor Lillie Mae Grissette and her late husband, Deacon Ray, thank you for opening up your home and hearts to me. Thank you for being my parents away from home.

To the late Pastor Fred and 1st Lady Lucille Holmes who always showed me other acts of kindness marriage that I hoped that one day I would get to experience. I was blessed to have him as my pastor for three years. He never changed who he was a loving, caring husband, father and grandfather.

To the late Pastor Willie James and 1st Lady Rosa Lee Hamilton, thank you for your loving spirits.

To the late Mr. James McDaniel (late Merdes) who always teased me about thinking that all marriages were like my parents and he was right I did think that.

To Aunt Caroline and Uncle Matthew (my father's sister and her husband) who are now deceased. They were very inspirational in us also seeing a loving marriage. They had a great love affair

To the late Deacon Wilson and Lurene Melvin, the late Bro. Bruce and Minister Sister Mattie Pearson, the late Rev. Eugene and Sister Tiny Simmons, the late Rev. Moses and Sister Eva Simmons, the late Mother Hattie Green.

To my late paternal grandparents, Willie and Maggie Singletary Frazier and my late maternal grandparents, James Lisbon and Charlotte White Cohen, without you all we would not be here today.

To late Mama Lela Richardson Manning who was the midwife that delivered six of my siblings and the godmother to us all. She lived on what was left of Badham Quarters.

To the late Deacon Floyd Johnson who spent so many countless hours at the Shoe Shop with Daddy and was a dear friend to him.

To the late Mr. Wesley Moorer who gave Daddy the land to build Shiloh. He saw the call that Daddy had and God touched his heart to sow it.

To the late(s) Deacon Clinton, Sr. and Pastor Mahalia Elmore, Minister Rebecca Haynes, Bro. David, Sr. and Pastor Lary, Pastor Hattie Boyd and all the saints that were with Daddy and MaDear at Shiloh the church that our father was founder and pastor.

To the late Bishop William and Christine Fuller Jr., Mother Laura M. Nichols, Bishop Nathaniel and First Lady Mary Roach, Deacon Floyd and Sister Grady Bell Johnson, Rev. Nelson Eady, Prophet Lee, Deacon English and Minister Mattie Dentley, Rev. Luther Alston, Rev. Andrew Singleton, Mother Flemma Mason Hopkins and all the saints that have gone on to be with the Lord, thank you for allowing our parents to observe your lives up close and personal.

To the late Minister Rosa Lee Elmore, who was Daddy's first member when he started his ministry. She was my husband's aunt.

To our mother's close friends the late(s) Mrs. Laura Mae Johnson, Mrs. Clara Lee Lewis, Mrs. Addie

DeLee Summers, Gradie Bell Johnson and their families.

To Danielle Fetherson (formerly Gilliard) a wonderful young lady who was very instrumental in getting this finished product. Thank you for helping me put everything together and making this book a reality.

To Joy Williams for sharing Danielle with us.

To Omar Fetherson for your unselfishness in allowing your wife to help others dream become a reality.

www.ingramcontent.com/pod-product-compliance
Lightning Source LLC
Chambersburg PA
CBHW050914160426
43194CB00011B/2404